Freezer Meal Recipes

Easy One-Pot Make Ahead Dump Meals

Louise Davidson

ISBN: 978-1981546091

Printed in the United States

Contents

Introduction

I believe that making assumptions is usually not the best idea. However, I am willing to bet that if you are looking at this book, then you have found yourself in the clutches of a busy modern family. Your family may consist of a dozen people or it might be you and a beloved pet. Regardless, your schedule is hectic, and you are looking for healthy, productive ways to streamline it, and maybe leave a little room for relaxation and pleasure at the end of a long day. I am also willing to guess that delicious food that nourishes both your body and spirit is a goal for you, but that there are days that it just doesn't all fit. It brings wonderful satisfaction to be able to help you achieve that goal with this collection of delicious freezer dump meals.

What exactly is a freezer dump meal? The concept is quite simple. Freezer cooking has become a popular trend recently. It is the act of preparing meals ahead of time and freezing them for later, so that all you need to do in order to enjoy a delicious home cooked meal is remove the dish from the freezer, cook, and eat. We have taken this concept one step further in this recipe collection and combined freezer cooking with the concept of dump cooking. Dump cooking is the process of adding all of your ingredients at once, maybe giving it a quick stir while cooking, but otherwise letting the dish take care of itself with very little fuss and attention required. Here we have created freezer meals that are prepared with minimal steps and no pre-freezer cooking required.

The Advantages of Freezer Dump Meals

First and foremost, freezer dump cooking saves time. These meals can prepared a month or two ahead of time, meaning that you always have a delicious meal made with fresh ingredients frozen at their prime at your fingertips whenever you want one. Many of the meals presented in this book are cooked using a slow cooker, which means that all you need to do is grab a meal and pop it in the slow cooker at the start of your day. You'll be rewarded with a wonderful, warm home-cooked meal hours later. That is it, no more than ten minutes of your time invested for a satisfying meal.

Freezer dump cooking is easy on your budget too. A little planning allows you to purchase fresh ingredients when they are at their seasonal peak and also their least expensive prices. Along with this is the money-saving aspect of convenience. How many times have you stopped at a drive-through or run into your grocery store on your way home to pick up a premade meal that was heavy on your gut and wallet? With freezer dump cooking, the need for that is eliminated. You get to save the money in your wallet while making healthier choices.

Freezer dump cooking keeps the end of your day less stressful. Not only are you not worrying about cooking, but the simple "dump and go" process means you will have nothing more than one pot or pan and your dinner dishes to clean up when it is all said and done. Your evenings can be spent relaxing rather than in the midst of kitchen chores.

Some Tricks to Make Freezer Dump Cooking Work for You

While this is one of the simplest preparation methods out there, here are a few tips to make preparing tasty home-cooked dump meals even easier.

1. Know your freezer space limit, and use the appropriately sized containers. You have several options for freezer containers including freezer bags and rigid plastic lidded containers. Be realistic concerning what you can fit in your freezer. If you are limited on freezer space, often freezer bags work best because they can be frozen flat and stored on top of each other. This can allow you to store ten meals in the same space that might only fit four or five lidded containers.

2. Meal Plan. This is both a time and money saver. Choose your favorite freezer dump meals and make a detailed list of what days you plan to have which meals. From their make your grocery list and make sure to make accommodations for singular dishes that you wish to double or triple for more than one meal. This will help you avoid unnecessary and costly additional trips to the grocery store.

3. Do it all in one day. If possible, choose one or two days during the month to prepare all of your freezer meals. This will free up more of your valuable time on a weekly and daily basis.

4. Thaw safely. You will want to thaw your freezer meals before cooking. For food safety reasons, do not leave your food out to thaw at room temperature. Instead, either remove the dish from the freezer the night before and thaw in the refrigerator for 12 hours or overnight, or use a microwave on the defrost setting to thaw the freezer packages.

5. Speaking of food safety, since the meat in these dishes is not precooked, make sure that any meat product reaches an internal temperature of 160°F/71°C. This is especially important if your meal was not completely thawed before cooking.

6. Finally, the method of cooking really is up to you. While many of the recipes in this collection are prepared in a slow cooker, there is no reason that you cannot use other methods of cooking for any singular dish. Freezer dump cooking is meant to make your life simpler. If something here doesn't work for you, it is very easy to modify it to suit your lifestyle.

You are now ready to enjoy these recipes. Happy cooking!

Beef Recipes

Mongolian Beef

Cook Time: 6 hours - Prep Time: 10 min - Servings: 4

Ingredients
1 pound flank steak, cut into strips
¼ cup cornstarch
1 teaspoon black pepper
1 teaspoon salt
1 teaspoon crushed red pepper
2 garlic cloves, crushed and minced
1 cup soy sauce
1 teaspoon sesame oil
1 cup brown sugar
1 cup water
2 cups broccoli florets
1 cup carrots, shredded
1 cup yellow onion, sliced
¼ cup scallions, for garnish if desired

Directions
1. Mix together the cornstarch, black pepper and salt in a bowl. Take the flank steak strips and toss them in the cornstarch mixture to coat well.
2. Place the steak strips in a large freezer storage bag or other container.
3. To the bag, add the crushed red pepper, garlic, soy sauce, sesame oil, brown sugar, water, broccoli, carrots, and yellow onion.
4. Seal the bag well and shake to mix the ingredients.
5. Serving day: Place contents in a slow cooker. Cook for 6-8 hours on medium to high if frozen, or thaw for 12 hours in the refrigerator, and cook for 4 hours on high.
6. Garnish with scallions, if desired.

Almost-Too-Tender Beef Ribs

Cook Time: 6-8 hours - Prep Time: 10 min - Servings: 4-6

Ingredients

2-3 pounds beef ribs
1 12-oz. can root beer
2 cups beef stock
½ cup tomato sauce
¼ cup Worcestershire sauce
¼ cup brown sugar
2 cups sweet potatoes, cubed
4 garlic cloves, crushed and minced
1 tablespoon fresh thyme
1 teaspoon salt
1 teaspoon pepper
1 cup yellow onions, sliced

Directions

1. Cut the beef ribs into pieces of 2-3 ribs each. Place them in one or two large freezer storage bags, or another freezer safe container.
2. In a bowl mix the root beer, beef stock, tomato sauce, Worcestershire sauce, brown sugar, garlic, thyme, salt, and pepper. Mix well.
3. Pour the marinade over the ribs, making sure that the meat is well coated.
4. Add the onions and sweet potatoes to the bag or container.
5. Serving Day: 12 hours before, remove the contents from the freezer and thaw in the refrigerator.
6. Place the contents into a slow cooker and cook for 6-8 hours on low.

Garlic and Rosemary Beef Stew

Cook Time: 6 hours - Prep Time: 10 min - Servings: 4-6

Ingredients

2 pounds beef stew meat

2 tablespoons cornstarch

1 ½ cups red onion, chopped

2 cups carrots, sliced

2 cups beets, cubed

6 garlic cloves, crushed and minced

3 cups beef stock

2 tablespoons honey

¼ cup Worcestershire sauce

2 sprigs fresh rosemary

1 teaspoon salt

2 teaspoons black pepper

Directions

1. Add the stew meat to a large freezer storage bag or other freezer safe container. Add in the cornstarch and toss to coat.
2. Add the red onion, carrots, beets and garlic. Shake to mix.
3. Pour in the beef stock, honey and Worcestershire sauce. Season with rosemary, salt and pepper.
4. Either stir or shake to ensure that all ingredients are well blended.
5. Place in the freezer until ready to use.
6. Serving Day: Remove from the freezer and thaw in the refrigerator for 12 hours. Place in a slow cooker and cook on low for 6-8 hours.

Soulful Beef Chili

Cook Time: 1 hour - Prep Time: 10 min - Servings: 4-6

Ingredients

1 pound beef stew meat
2 15-oz cans pinto beans, drained
2 15-oz cans stewed tomatoes, liquid reserved
1 15-oz can yellow hominy, drained
1 cup yellow onion, diced
3 cups tomato juice
2 cups beef broth
½ cup poblano pepper, diced
4 garlic cloves, crushed and minced
2 teaspoons cocoa powder
2 teaspoons molasses
1 tablespoon crushed red pepper flakes
2 teaspoons smoky paprika
2 teaspoons chili powder
1 teaspoon onion powder
1 teaspoon salt
1 teaspoon black pepper

Directions

1. Add the stew meat, pinto beans, stewed tomatoes with liquid, hominy, and yellow onion to a large freezer bag or other storage container.
2. Pour in the tomato juice and beef broth. Add the poblano pepper, garlic, cocoa powder, and molasses. Mix well.
3. Season with crushed red pepper, smoky paprika, chili powder, onion powder, salt and pepper. Mix again and seal tightly. Place in the freezer until ready to use.
4. Serving Day: Take package out of the freezer and let frost for 12 hours in the refrigerator.
5. Place the contents in a large stockpot and bring to a boil. Boil for 5 minutes before covering and reducing heat to low.
6. Simmer for 1 hour or until meat is cooked through,

Beef Enchilada Bake

Cook Time: 40 min - Prep Time: 10 min - Servings: 4

Ingredients

1 pound shredded cooked beef
2 cups fresh corn kernels
1 cup red onion, diced
1 cup red bell pepper, diced
3 garlic cloves, crushed and minced
1 8-oz can tomato sauce
1 cup beef broth
1 tablespoon chili powder
½ teaspoon cumin
1 teaspoon salt
1 teaspoon pepper
1 cup queso cheese, shredded
4-6 corn tortillas (for serving day)

Directions

1. Add the shredded beef, corn, red onion, red bell pepper, and garlic to a large freezer bag or other storage container.
2. In a small bowl combine the tomato sauce, beef broth, chili powder, cumin, salt, and pepper. Whisk well, and pour over the shredded beef.
3. Add the queso cheese, mix well and seal the container tightly before placing in the freezer.
4. Serving Day: Remove the package from the freezer and allow thawing for 12 hours in the refrigerator.
5. Preheat oven to 350°F/177°C.
6. Pour half of the contents into a 9"x9" baking dish. Place a layer of corn tortillas over the mix, followed by the remaining contents.
7. Place in the oven, and bake for 30-40 minutes or until heated through.

Tender Red Wine Beef Steaks

Cook Time: 6 hours - Prep Time: 10 min - Servings: 4

Ingredients

4 beef sirloin steaks, 4-6 oz. each
2 cups broccoli florets, chopped
1 cup fresh snow peas
1 cup red onion, sliced
2 garlic cloves, crushed and minced
1 ½ cups red wine
½ cup olive oil
¼ cup Worcestershire sauce
1 tablespoon fresh thyme
1 sprig fresh rosemary
1 teaspoon salt
1 teaspoon pepper

Directions

1. Place the sirloin steaks, broccoli, snow peas, red onion and garlic in a large freezer bag or other storage container.
2. In a bowl combine the red wine, olive oil, Worcestershire sauce, thyme, rosemary, salt and pepper. Pour contents over the steak.
3. Seal the container well and place in the freezer.
4. Serving Day: Remove the contents from the freezer and thaw for 12 hours in the refrigerator.
5. Place the steak, vegetables, and marinade in a slow cooker and cook on low for 6 hours.
6. Remove rosemary sprig before serving.

Italian Beef and Mushrooms

Cook Time: 35 min - Prep Time: 10 min - Servings: 4

Ingredients

1 pound beef stew meat
2 cups portabella mushrooms, cut into chunks
2 heirloom tomatoes, chopped
2 garlic cloves, crushed and minced
2 cups fresh green beans, trimmed
1 cup tomato juice
½ cup dry red wine
2 teaspoons oregano
2 tablespoons fresh basil
1 fresh rosemary sprig
1 teaspoon salt
1 teaspoon pepper

Directions

1. Add the stew meat, portabella mushrooms, tomatoes, garlic, and green beans to a large freezer bag or other storage container.
2. Add in the tomato juice, red wine, oregano, basil, rosemary, salt and pepper.
3. Seal tightly and place in the freezer.
4. Serving Day: Remove the contents from the freezer and let thaw in the refrigerator for 12 hours.
5. Place the contents in a large skillet and heat over medium-high for 5 minutes.
6. Reduce the heat to a simmer, cover, and cook for 30-35 minutes or until meat is cooked through.

Inside Out Sheppard's Pie

Cook Time: 40 min - Prep Time: 10 min - Servings: 4

Ingredients

1 pound ground crumbled ground beef
1 cup carrots, diced
2 cups fresh peas
1 cup yellow onion, diced
2 garlic cloves, crushed and minced
2 teaspoons tomato paste
1 cup beef stock
1 tablespoon Worcestershire sauce
2 teaspoons thyme
1 sprig fresh rosemary
1 teaspoon salt
1 teaspoon black pepper

Directions

1. In a large freezer bag or other storage container, combine the ground beef, carrots, peas, onion, and garlic.
2. In a small bowl combine the tomato paste, beef stock, Worcestershire sauce, thyme, rosemary, salt, and black pepper. Mix well.
3. Pour the liquid over the meat and vegetables. Seal the container tightly and place in the freezer.
4. Serving Day: Remove the contents from the freezer and thaw for 12 hours in the refrigerator.
5. Preheat oven to 375°F/191°C.
6. Place the contents in an 8"x8" baking dish. Place in the oven and bake for 35-40 minutes, or until meat is cooked through.
7. Serve warm.

Chicken Recipes

At the Family Ranch Chicken

Cook Time: 6 hours - Prep Time: 10 min - Servings: 4

Ingredients
4 boneless, skinless chicken breasts
2 cups black beans (canned or pre-cooked)
2 cups fresh corn kernels
1 cup red onion, diced
3 garlic cloves, crushed and minced
1 ½ cups buttermilk
1 cup mayonnaise
¼ cup fresh parsley
¼ cup fresh chives
2 tablespoons fresh dill
1 teaspoon salt
1 teaspoon black pepper
1 tablespoon sliced scallions, for garnish

Directions
1. Place the chicken, black beans, corn kernels, red onion, and garlic in a large freezer bag or other storage container.
2. In a small bowl mix together the buttermilk, mayonnaise, parsley, chives, dill, salt, and black pepper. Mix well.
3. Pour the mixture over the chicken, beans and vegetables. Seal the container tightly and place in the freezer.
4. Serving Day: Remove the contents from the freezer and thaw in the refrigerator for 12 hours.
5. Place the contents in a slow cooker and cook on low for 6 hours or until chicken is cooked though and juices run clear.
6. Garnish with fresh scallions, if desired.

Old World Chicken Cacciatore

Cook Time: 8 hours - Prep Time: 10 min - Servings: 4

Ingredients
8 chicken breasts and thighs
½ cup red onion, diced
1 cup green bell pepper, cubed
1 cup red bell pepper, cubed
3 garlic cloves, crushed and minced
1 28-oz can crushed tomatoes, liquid reserved
½ cup dry red wine
¼ cup fresh basil
2 tablespoons fresh oregano
1 bay leaf
1 teaspoon salt
1 teaspoon black pepper
Fresh, grated parmesan cheese, for garnish

Directions
1. Place the chicken breast in a large freezer bag or other storage container.
2. Add in the red onion, green bell pepper, red bell pepper and garlic
3. In a bowl combine the tomatoes, with the liquid, dry red wine, basil, oregano, bay leaf, salt and black pepper. Mix well.
4. Pour over the chicken and vegetables. Seal the container and place in the freezer.
5. Serving Day: Remove the contents from the freezer and thaw for 12 hours in the refrigerator.
6. Place the contents in a slow cooker and cook on low for 8 hours, or until chicken is cooked through and juices run clear.
7. Garnish with fresh grated parmesan, if desired.

Garlicky Honey Chicken

Cook Time: 35 min - Prep Time: 10 min - Servings: 4

Ingredients

4 boneless, skinless chicken breasts
¼ pound bacon, cubed
2 cups green beans, trimmed
1 cup yellow onion, diced
5 garlic cloves, crushed and minced
1 cup chicken stock
¼ cup olive oil
¼ cup honey
1 teaspoon paprika
1 teaspoon salt
1teaspoon black pepper
Sliced almonds, for garnish if desired

Directions

1. Place the chicken, bacon, green beans, yellow onion, and garlic in a large freezer bag or other storage container.
2. In a bowl combine the chicken stock, olive oil, honey, paprika, salt, and pepper.
3. Pour the mixture over the chicken and seal the container tightly. Place in the freezer.
4. Serving Day: Remove the contents from the freezer and thaw in the refrigerator for 12 hours.
5. Place the contents in a large skillet and cook over medium high for 5 minutes or until liquid begins to bubble.
6. Cover skillet, reduce heat to medium low, and cook for 25-30 minutes or until chicken is cooked through and juices run clear.
7. Garnish with almonds before serving, if desired.

Maple Mustard Chicken

Cook Time: 8 hours - Prep Time: 10 min - Servings: 4-6

Ingredients

8 pieces bone-in chicken breasts and thighs
4 cups Brussels sprouts, halves
1 cup leeks, cleaned and sliced
3 garlic cloves, crushed and minced
1 cup chicken stock
¼ cup olive oil
¼ pure maple syrup
1 tablespoon Dijon mustard
1 sprig fresh rosemary
1 teaspoon salt
2 teaspoons coarse ground black pepper

Directions

1. Place the chicken pieces, Brussels sprouts, leeks, and garlic in a large freezer bag or other storage container.
2. In a bowl, combine the chicken stock, olive oil, maple syrup, and Dijon mustard. Whisk well and pour into container over chicken.
3. Season with rosemary, salt, and black pepper. Seal the container tightly and place in the freezer.
4. Serving Day: Remove the contents from the freezer and thaw in the refrigerator for at least 12 hours.
5. Place the contents in a slow cooker and cook on low for 8 hours or until chicken is cooked through and juices run clear.

Herby Chicken Alfredo

Cook Time: 6 hours - Prep Time: 10 min - Servings: 4

Ingredients
4 boneless, skinless chicken breasts
3 cups broccoli florets
1 ½ cups mushrooms, halved
2 cups fresh spinach, torn
4 garlic cloves, crushed and minced
1 cup chicken broth
1 ½ cups heavy cream
¼ cup melted butter
½ cup freshly grated parmesan cheese
½ cup fresh parsley, chopped
½ cup fresh basil, chopped
1 teaspoon salt
1 teaspoon black pepper
Cooked pasta or rice for serving (optional)

Directions
1. Place the chicken, broccoli, mushrooms, spinach, and garlic in a large freezer bag or other storage container.
2. In a bowl combine the chicken broth, heavy cream and melted butter. Whisk until blended.
3. Add in the parmesan cheese, parsley, basil, salt, and black pepper. Pour the contents over the chicken.
4. Seal the container tightly and place in the freezer.
5. Serving Day: Remove the contents from the freezer and thaw in the refrigerator for at least 12 hours.
6. Place the contents in a slow cooker and cook on low for 6 hours, or until chicken is cooked through and juices run clear.
7. Serve with cooked rice or pasta, if desired.

West Coast Chicken

Cook Time: 35 min - Prep Time: 10 min - Servings: 4

Ingredients
4 boneless, skinless chicken breasts
2 cups green beans, trimmed
1 cup onion, sliced
2 garlic cloves, crushed and minced
1 jalapeno pepper, diced
½ cup orange juice
¼ cup lime juice
¼ cup olive oil
1 tablespoon orange zest
1 teaspoon lime zest
1 tablespoon honey
1 teaspoon coriander
1 teaspoon salt
1 teaspoon pepper
Cooked rice for serving (optional)

Directions
1. Place the chicken, green beans, onion, garlic, and jalapeno pepper in a large freezer bag or other storage container.
2. In a small bowl combine the orange juice, lime juice, olive oil, orange zest, lime zest, honey, coriander, salt, and pepper. Whisk well.
3. Pour the liquid over the chicken. Seal the container tightly and place in the freezer.
4. Serving Day: Remove the contents from the freezer and thaw in the refrigerator for 12 hours.
5. Place the contents in a large skillet and cook over medium high heat for 5 minutes.
6. Reduce heat to medium-low and cook for an additional 25-30 minutes, or until chicken is cooked through and juices run clear.
7. Serve with cooked rice, if desired.

Lemon Poppy Seed Chicken

Cook Time: 8 hours - Prep Time: 10 min - Servings: 4-6

Ingredients

8 pieces bone-in chicken breast and thighs
3 cups broccoli florets
1 cup fresh peas
½ cup yellow onion, diced
2 garlic cloves, crushed and minced
¼ cup preserved lemons, chopped
1 cup lemon juice
¼ cup olive oil
1 tablespoon fresh tarragon
1 tablespoon poppy seeds
1 teaspoon salt
2 teaspoons coarse ground black pepper

Directions

1. Place the chicken, broccoli, peas, onion and garlic in a large freezer bag or other storage container.
2. In a bowl combine the preserved lemons, lemon juice, olive oil, tarragon, poppy seeds, salt and black pepper. Mix well.
3. Pour the liquid over the chicken and seal the container tightly. Place in the freezer.
4. Serving Day: Remove the contents from the freezer and thaw in the refrigerator for at least 12 hours.
5. Place the contents in a slow cooker and cook on low for 8 hours or until chicken is cooked through and juices run clear.

Double Peppered Chicken

Cook Time: 35 min - Prep Time: 10 min - Servings: 4

Ingredients
4 boneless, skinless chicken breasts
1 cup red bell pepper, sliced
1 cup green bell pepper, sliced
1 cup yellow onion, sliced
¼ cup soy sauce
¼ rice vinegar
1 tablespoon honey
1 tablespoon fresh grated ginger
1 tablespoon crushed red pepper flakes
1 teaspoon salt
2 teaspoons coarse ground black pepper

Directions
1. Place the chicken, red bell pepper, green bell pepper and yellow onion in a large freezer bag or other storage container.
2. In a bowl combine the soy sauce, rice vinegar, honey, ginger, red pepper flakes, salt, and black pepper. Seal the container and place in the freezer.
3. Serving Day: Remove the contents from the freezer and thaw in the refrigerator for 12 hours.
4. Place the contents in a large skillet and heat over medium high for 5 minutes.
5. Reduce the heat to medium low and cook for an additional 25-30 minutes or until chicken is cooked through and juices run clear.

Chicken Kiev Bake

Cook Time: 45 min - Prep Time: 10 min - Servings: 4-6

Ingredients

8 pieces bone-in chicken breast and thighs
3 cups broccoli florets
1 cup yellow onion, sliced
2 garlic cloves, crushed and minced
½ cup butter, cubed
½ cup fresh parsley
¼ cup fresh tarragon
1 teaspoon salt
1 teaspoon black pepper
1 cup seasoned panko bread crumbs

Directions

1. Place the chicken, broccoli, onions, garlic and butter in a large freezer bag or other storage container.
2. Season with parsley, tarragon, salt, black pepper and bread crumbs. Toss the ingredients in the bag to mix. Seal tightly and place in the freezer.
3. Serving Day: Remove the contents from the freezer and thaw in the refrigerator for 12 hours.
4. Preheat the oven to 375°F/191°C.
5. Empty the contents into a lightly oiled baking dish. Cover with aluminum foil and place in the oven.
6. Bake for 45-50 minutes or until chicken is cooked through and juices run clear.

Sticky BBQ Chicken

Cook Time: 8 hours - Prep Time: 10 min - Servings: 4-6

Ingredients

8 pieces bone-in chicken breasts and thighs
2 cups carrots, sliced
1 cup canned pineapple, drained
4 ears fresh corn, quartered
½ cup ketchup
¼ cup brown sugar
½ cup apple juice
2 tablespoons orange juice
1 tablespoon bourbon whisky
1 tablespoon Worcestershire sauce
1 tablespoon Dijon mustard
1 tablespoon paprika
1 teaspoon ground cumin
2 teaspoons fennel seeds
1 teaspoon salt
1 teaspoon black pepper

Directions

1. Place the chicken in large freezer bag or other storage container.
2. In a bowl combine the ketchup, brown sugar, apple juice, orange juice, bourbon whisky, Worcestershire sauce, Dijon mustard, paprika, cumin, fennel, salt and black pepper. Mix well.
3. Pour the sauce over the chicken and toss to coat.
4. Add the carrots, pineapple, and corn to the bag and seal tightly. Place in the freezer.
5. Serving Day: Remove the container from the freezer and thaw in the refrigerator for at least 12 hours.
6. Place the contents in a slow cooker and cook over low heat for 8 hours or until chicken is cooked through and juices run clear.

Pork Recipes

Peppery Pulled Pork

Cook Time: 8 hours - Prep Time: 10 min - Servings: 6-8

Ingredients
1 4 to 6-pounds pork roast
2 cups yellow onion, sliced
4 garlic cloves, crushed and minced
¼ cup olive oil
¼ cup rice vinegar
1 tablespoon Dijon mustard
1 tablespoon honey
2 tablespoons black peppercorns
1 tablespoon chili powder
1 tablespoon smoked paprika
2 teaspoons cumin
1 teaspoon coriander
1 teaspoon salt
Sandwich buns for serving (optional)

Directions
1. Add the pork roast, onions, and garlic to a large freezer bag or other storage container.
2. In a bowl combine the olive oil, rice vinegar, Dijon mustard. Honey, black peppercorns, chili powder, smoked paprika, cumin, coriander, and salt. Mix well.
3. Pour the marinade over the pork. Seal the container tightly and place in the freezer.
4. Serving Day: Remove the contents from the freezer and thaw in the refrigerator 12-16 hours.
5. Place the contents in a slow cooker and cook over low heat for 8 hours or until pork measures an internal temperature of 160°F/71°C.
6. Shred the pork roast before serving.
7. Serve on sandwich buns, if desired

Orange Pork and Rice

Cook Time: 6 hours - Prep Time: 10 min - Servings: 4

Ingredients

1 ½-pounds pork stir fry meat
2 cups broccoli florets
2 cups snow peas, trimmed
¼ cup shallots, sliced
3 garlic cloves, crushed and minced
1 cup chicken stock
1 cup orange marmalade
¼ cup soy sauce
2 tablespoons Dijon mustard
2 tablespoons honey
1 teaspoon salt
1 teaspoon pepper
4 cups cooked rice
Scallions, sliced for garnish

Directions

1. Place the pork, broccoli florets, snow peas, scallions, and garlic in a large freezer bag or other storage container.
2. In a bowl combine the chicken stock, orange marmalade, soy sauce, Dijon mustard, honey, salt, and pepper. Mix well.
3. Pour the marinade over the pork and vegetables. Add the rice to the bag, seal tightly and place in the freezer.
4. Serving Day: Remove the contents from the freezer and thaw for 12 hours.
5. Place the contents in a slow cooker and cook for 4-6 hours on medium heat.
6. Garnish with fresh scallions, if desired.

Spicy, Cilantro Lime Pork

Cook Time: 30 min - Prep Time: 10 min - Servings: 4

Ingredients

4 pork chops, approximately 6 oz each
2 cups green bell peppers, sliced
1 cup yellow bell pepper, sliced
1 cup yellow onion, sliced
2 ears fresh corn, quartered
2 garlic cloves, crushed and minced
1 jalapeno pepper, diced
¼ cup olive oil
1 cup chicken stock
¼ cup fresh lime juice
1 teaspoon honey
1 tablespoon cayenne pepper sauce
½ cup fresh cilantro, chopped
1 teaspoon salt
1 teaspoon black pepper
Cooked rice for serving (optional)

Directions

1. Place the pork, green bell pepper, yellow bell pepper, onion, corn quarters, garlic and jalapeno pepper in a large freezer bag or other storage container.
2. In a bowl combine the olive oil, chicken stock, lime juice, honey, cayenne pepper sauce, cilantro, salt, and black pepper. Mix well.
3. Pour the liquid into the bag and seal tightly. Place the contents into the freezer.
4. Serving Day: Remove the contents from the freezer and thaw in the refrigerator for 12 hours.
5. Place the contents into a large skillet and heat over medium high for 5 minutes. Reduce heat to medium and cook for 20-25 minutes or until pork is cooked though.
6. Serve with cooked rice, if desired.

Smothered Pork Chops

Cook Time: 6 hours - Prep Time: 10 min - Servings: 4

Ingredients

4 bone-in pork chops
2 cups yellow onions, sliced
2 cups mushrooms, sliced
2 cups acorn squash, quartered
4 garlic cloves, crushed and minced
1 cup chicken stock
1 cup buttermilk
½ cup cream cheese, cut into small cubes
2 teaspoons paprika
1 teaspoon sage
1 teaspoon salt
2 teaspoons ground black pepper
1 fresh rosemary sprig

Directions

1. Place the pork, onions, mushrooms, acorn squash and garlic in a large freezer bag or other storage container.
2. In a bowl combine the chicken stock, buttermilk, cream cheese, paprika, sage, salt, and black pepper. Mix well and pour into the bag.
3. Add the fresh rosemary, seal the bag, and place in the freezer.
4. Serving Day: Remove the contents from the freezer and thaw in the refrigerator for 12 hours.
5. Place in the slow cooker and cook on low for 6-8 hours or until pork is cooked through and internal temperature measures 160°F/71°C.

Citrus Tenderloin Roast

Cook Time: 6-8 hours - Prep Time: 10 min - Servings: 6-8

Ingredients

1 4 to 5-pounds pork tenderloin roast
2 cups fennel, sliced
2 cups carrots, sliced
2 garlic cloves, crushed and minced
1 cup onion, sliced
½ orange, sliced
½ cup orange juice
¼ cup lime juice
¼ cup dry cooking sherry
½ cup chicken stock
2 tablespoons olive oil
¼ cup fresh parsley, chopped
1 teaspoon coriander
1 teaspoon salt
1 teaspoon black pepper

Directions

1. Place the pork, fennel, carrots, garlic, onion, and orange slices in a large freezer bag or other storage container.
2. In a bowl combine the orange juice, lime juice, cooking sherry, chicken stock, olive oil, parsley, coriander, salt, and black pepper. Mix well.
3. Pour the marinade over the pork and vegetables. Seal the container tightly and place in the freezer.
4. Serving Day: Remove the contents from the freezer and thaw in the refrigerator for 12-16 hours.
5. Place in the slow cooker and cook on low heat for 6-8 hours or until pork is cooked through and measures an internal temperature of 160°F/71°C.

29

Pork Medallions with Shallot Sauce

Cook Time: 25 min - Prep Time: 10 min - Servings: 6

Ingredients

1 ½-pounds pork tenderloin, sliced into medallions
2 cups mushrooms, sliced
1 cup fresh peas
¼ cup shallots, sliced
¼ cup balsamic vinegar
1 cup chicken stock
¼ cup olive oil
1 tablespoon brown sugar
1 teaspoon thyme
1 teaspoon salt
1 teaspoon black pepper

Directions

1. Place the pork medallions, mushrooms, and peas in a large freezer bag or other storage container.
2. In a bowl combine the shallots, balsamic vinegar, chicken stock, olive oil, brown sugar, thyme, salt, and black pepper. Mix well.
3. Pour the shallot sauce over the pork. Seal the container tightly and place in the freezer.
4. Serving Day: Remove the contents from the freezer and thaw in the refrigerator for 12 hours.
5. Place the contents in a large skillet and cook over medium high heat for 3-5 minutes or until sauce reduces slightly.
6. Reduce heat to a medium-low simmer and cook for 20 minutes or until pork medallions are cooked through.

Jerk Pork Tenderloin

Cook Time: 1 hour - Prep Time: 10 min - Servings: 6

Ingredients
1 pork tenderloin roast, approximately 1 ½ pounds
1 cup yellow onion, sliced
1 15-oz can pineapple chunks, liquid reserved
1 cup red pepper, sliced
1 ½ cups sweet potatoes, cubed
4 garlic cloves, crushed and minced
1 Serrano pepper, minced
1 ½ cups chicken stock
½ cup apple cider
1 tablespoon honey
1 tablespoon fresh grated ginger
½ teaspoon cinnamon
1 teaspoon allspice
½ teaspoon nutmeg
1 teaspoon salt
1 teaspoon black pepper
Scallions, sliced for garnish

Directions
1. Place the tenderloin, yellow onion, pineapple chunks, red pepper, and sweet potatoes in a large freezer bag or other storage container.
2. In a bowl combine the remaining pineapple liquid, garlic, Serrano pepper, chicken stock, apple cider, honey, ginger, cinnamon, allspice, nutmeg, salt, and black pepper. Mix well.
3. Pour the liquid into the bag and seal tightly. Place in the freezer.
4. Serving Day: Remove the contents from the freezer and thaw in the refrigerator for 12-16 hours.
5. Preheat the oven to 350°F/177°C
6. Place the contents in a roasting pan and place in the oven. Roast for 55-60 minutes or until pork is cooked through in the center.
7. Garnish with scallions, if desired.

BBQ Rib Tips

Cook Time: 6 hours - Prep Time: 10 min - Servings: 4-6

Ingredients
2 pounds pork rib tips
2 cups red bell pepper, sliced
1 cup onion, sliced
2 garlic cloves, crushed and minced
1 teaspoon chili powder
1 teaspoon rubbed sage
1 teaspoon salt
1 teaspoon black pepper
½ cup ketchup
½ cup brown sugar
2 tablespoons apple cider vinegar
2 teaspoons dry mustard
1 tablespoon Worcestershire sauce
1 teaspoon cinnamon

Directions
1. Place the rib tips in a large freezer bag or other storage container. Season the meat with the chili powder, rubbed sage, salt, and black pepper.
2. Add the red pepper, onion, and garlic to the bag.
3. In a bowl combine the ketchup, brown sugar, apple cider vinegar, dry mustard, Worcestershire sauce, and cinnamon. Mix well.
4. Pour the sauce over the rib tips. Seal the container tightly and place in the freezer.
5. Serving Day: Remove the contents from the freezer and thaw in the refrigerator for 12 hours.
6. Place the contents in a slow cooker and cook on low for 6-8 hours until cooked through and tender.

Seafood Recipes

Green Chili Seafood Stew

Cook Time: 25 min - Prep Time: 10 min - Servings: 6

Ingredients

1 pound whitefish fillets, cubed

½ pound salmon fillet, cubed

½ pound shrimp, peeled and deveined

1 cup yellow onion, diced

4 garlic cloves, crushed and minced

½ cup poblano pepper, diced

¼ cup canned green chilies

1 cup oyster mushrooms, chopped

2 ears corn, quartered

2 cups collard greens, torn

1 cup fresh parsley, chopped

¼ cup fresh cilantro, chopped

8 cups fish stock

2 tablespoons fish sauce

1 tablespoon lemon juice

1 teaspoon chili powder

1 teaspoon salt

1 teaspoon black pepper

Lemon wedges for garnish

Directions

1. Combine the whitefish, salmon, and shrimp in a large freezer bag or other storage container.
2. Add the yellow onion, garlic, poblano pepper, green chilies, mushrooms, corn, and collard greens. Toss to mix.

33

3. In a bowl combine the parsley, cilantro, fish stock, fish sauce, lemon juice, chili powder, salt, and black pepper. Mix well.
4. Pour the broth into the container. Seal tightly and place in the freezer.
5. Serving Day: Remove the contents from the freezer and thaw in the refrigerator for 12 hours.
6. Place the contents in a large stockpot. Bring to a light boil over medium high heat for 3-5 minutes.
7. Reduce heat to low, cover and simmer for 20 minutes.
8. Garnish with fresh lemon wedges, if desired.

Salmon with Sesame Marinade

Cook Time: 15 min - Prep Time: 10 min - Servings: 4

Ingredients
4 salmon filets, approximately 4-6 oz each
2 cups broccoli florets
1 cup edamame, shelled
¼ cup soy sauce
¼ cup rice vinegar
2 tablespoons sesame oil
1 teaspoon cayenne pepper sauce
¼ cup brown sugar
1 tablespoon fresh grated ginger
2 garlic cloves, crushed and minced
1 tablespoon sesame seeds

Directions
1. Combine the salmon, broccoli, and edamame in a large freezer bag or other storage container.
2. In a bowl combine the soy sauce, rice vinegar, sesame oil, cayenne pepper sauce, sugar, fresh ginger, garlic, and sesame seeds. Mix well.
3. Pour the marinade over the salmon. Seal the container tightly and place in the freezer.
4. Serving Day: Remove the contents from the freezer and thaw in the refrigerator for 12 hours.
5. Add a small amount of oil to a large sauté pan.
6. Gently push the vegetables to the side of the sauté pan so that the salmon is in the center.
7. Empty the contents into the pan and cook over medium heat for 10 minutes, flipping the salmon once halfway through.
8. Bring the vegetables back into the center of the pan over the salmon. Cook for an additional 2-5 minutes or until salmon is pink and flakey in the center.

Lemonade Whitefish

Cook Time: 15 min - Prep Time: 10 min - Servings: 4

Ingredients
1 pound whitefish filets
2 cups green beans, trimmed
1 cup fennel, sliced
2 garlic cloves, crushed and minced
1 cup chicken stock
1 cup fresh lemonade
1 tablespoon whole peppercorns
1 teaspoon salt
1 teaspoon black pepper
1 sprig fresh rosemary
Fresh lemon wedges for garnish

Directions
1. Place the whitefish, green beans, fennel, and garlic in a large freezer bag or other storage container.
2. In a bowl combine the chicken stock, lemonade, peppercorns, salt, and pepper. Pour the liquid over the fish.
3. Add the sprig of rosemary and seal the container tightly. Place in the freezer.
4. Serving Day: Remove the contents from the freezer and thaw in the refrigerator for 12 hours.
5. Lightly oil a large skillet and empty the freezer bag into the pan. Heat over medium-high for 3-5 minutes or until liquid begins to bubble.
6. Reduce heat to medium-low and cook for an additional 10 minutes or until fish is cooked through and vegetables are crisp tender.
7. Serve with fresh lemon wedges as a garnish, if desired.

Aloha Shrimp

Cook Time: 15 min - Prep Time: 10 min - Servings: 4

Ingredients

1 ½ pounds shrimp, peeled and deveined
1 cup red onion diced
1 cup red bell pepper, chopped
1 15-oz can pineapple chunks, liquid reserved
3 garlic cloves, crushed and minced
¼ cup butter, cubed
1 tablespoon crushed red pepper flakes
2 tablespoons unsweetened shredded coconut
1 tablespoon fresh lemongrass, chopped
1 teaspoon salt
1 teaspoon black pepper
Cooked rice for serving (optional)

Directions

1. In a large freezer bag or other storage container combine the shrimp, red onion, red bell pepper, and pineapple chunks.
2. Combine the reserved pineapple liquid with the garlic, cubed butter, red pepper flakes, coconut, lemongrass, salt, and black pepper. Mix well and pour over the shrimp.
3. Seal the container tightly and place in the freezer.
4. Serving Day: Remove the contents from the freezer and thaw in the refrigerator for 12 hours.
5. Add the contents to a large sauté pan and heat over medium high heat for 3-5 minutes.
6. Reduce heat to medium and cook for an additional 7-10 minutes or until shrimp is cooked through.
7. Serve with cooked rice if desired.

Italian Seafood Stew

Cook Time: 30 min - Prep Time: 10 min - Servings: 6

Ingredients
½ pound salmon filet, cubed
½ pound halibut, cubed
½ pound scallops
1 cup red onion, diced
1 cup fennel, chopped
2 cups zucchini, cubed
5 garlic cloves, crushed and minced
1 28-oz can crushed tomatoes, including liquid
4 cups fish stock
2 tablespoons tomato paste
1 tablespoon crushed red pepper
½ cup fresh parsley, chopped
½ cup fresh basil, chopped
1 bay leaf
1 teaspoon salt
1 teaspoon black pepper

Directions
1. Place the salmon, halibut, scallops, red onion, fennel, and zucchini in a large freezer bag or other storage container.
2. In a bowl combine the garlic, canned tomatoes, fish stock, and tomato paste. Mix well.
3. Season the broth with crushed red pepper, parsley, basil, bay leaf, salt and black pepper. Pour the broth over the fish and vegetables and seal the container tightly. Place in the freezer.
4. Serving Day: Remove the contents from the freezer and thaw in the refrigerator for 12 hours.
5. Empty the contents into a large stock pot. Heat over medium-high just until broth begins to bubble. Reduce heat to low and simmer for 20-25 minutes or until fish is cooked through and vegetables are firm tender.

Vegetarian Recipes

Curry Vegetables and Chickpeas

Cook Time: 4 hours - Prep Time: 10 min - Servings: 4-6

Ingredients
2 cups chickpeas (canned or previously cooked)
1 cup yellow onion, diced
2 cups sweet potatoes, cubed
1 cup carrots, chopped
2 cups green beans, trimmed
3 garlic cloves, crushed and minced
4 cups fresh spinach, torn
1 cup tomatoes, diced
1 jalapeno pepper, diced
1 tablespoon fresh grated ginger
2 cups vegetable stock
1 cup tomato juice
1 cup coconut milk
1 tablespoon curry powder
2 teaspoons honey
¼ cup fresh basil, chopped
¼ cup fresh lemongrass, chopped
1 teaspoon salt
1 teaspoon black pepper
Cooked rice for serving (optional)

Directions
1. In a large freezer bag or other storage container combine the chickpeas, onion, sweet potatoes, carrots, green beans, garlic, spinach, tomatoes, jalapeno pepper, and ginger. Toss to mix.
2. In a bowl combine the vegetable stock, tomato juice, coconut milk, curry powder, honey, basil, lemongrass, salt, and black pepper. Mix well.

3. Pour the broth over the vegetables. Seal the container tightly and place it in the freezer.
4. Serving Day: Remove the contents from the freezer and thaw in the refrigerator for 12 hours, or thaw in a microwave on the defrost setting.
5. Empty the contents into a slow cooker. Cook on low heat for 4-6 hours.
6. Serve with cooked rice, if desired

Four Bean Chili

Cook Time: 6 hours - Prep Time: 10 min - Servings: 6

Ingredients
1 15-oz can black beans
1 15-oz can kidney beans
1 15-oz can pinto beans
1 cup red onion, chopped
2 cups fresh corn kernels
1 red bell pepper, diced
1 tablespoon jalapeno pepper, diced
½ cup poblano pepper, diced
4 garlic cloves, crushed and minced
1 cup refried beans
2 cups vegetable stock
2 cups spicy tomato juice
½ cup dark beer
3 tablespoons chili powder
1 tablespoon ground cumin
1 tablespoon smoky paprika
2 teaspoons cocoa powder
1 teaspoon salt
Scallions, sliced for garnish
Monterey Jack cheese, shredded for garnish (optional)

Directions
1. Combine the black beans, kidney beans, pinto beans, red onion, corn, bell pepper, jalapeno pepper, poblano pepper, and garlic in a large freezer bag or other storage container.
2. In a bowl combine the refried beans, vegetable stock, spicy tomato juice, dark beer, chili powder, cumin, smoky paprika, cocoa powder, and salt. Mix well until refried beans are blended in.

41

3. Pour the liquid in the container and seal tightly. Place in the freezer.
4. Serving Day: Remove the contents from the freezer and thaw in the refrigerator for 12 hours or thaw in a microwave on the defrost setting.
5. Pour the contents into a slow cooker and cook on low for 6 hours.
6. Garnish with fresh scallions and cheese, if desired

Vegetable Barley Soup

Cook Time: 6 hours - Prep Time: 10 min - Servings: 6

Ingredients

1 cup uncooked barley

1 cup red onion, chopped

1 cup carrots, chopped

1 cup celery, chopped

1 cup green beans, trimmed

3 garlic cloves, crushed and minced

2 cups kidney beans (canned or previously cooked)

1 15-oz can stewed tomatoes, liquid reserved

8 cups vegetable stock

½ cup fresh parsley chopped

1 tablespoon fresh thyme

1 bay leaf

1 teaspoon salt

1 teaspoon black pepper

Directions

1. Combine the barley, red onion, carrots, celery, green beans, garlic, kidney beans and tomatoes in a large freezer bag or other storage container.
2. In a large bowl combine the reserved liquid from the tomatoes with the vegetable stock, parsley, thyme, bay leaf, salt, and black pepper. Mix well.
3. Pour the broth in with the vegetables. Seal the container tightly and store in the freezer.
4. Serving Day: Remove the contents from the freezer and thaw in the refrigerator for 12 hours, or thaw in a microwave on the defrost setting.
5. Add the contents to a slow cooker and cook on low for 6 hours, or until barley is cooked and tender.

Hearty Greens with Bean Medley

Cook Time: 25 min - Prep Time: 10 min - Servings: 4-6

Ingredients

3 cups cannellini beans (canned or previously cooked)
2 cups kale, chopped
2 cups collard greens, chopped
1 cup red onion, diced
1 cup tomato, diced
4 garlic cloves, crushed and minced
4 cups vegetable stock
1 tablespoon fresh lemon juice
2 teaspoons crushed red pepper flakes
1 tablespoon fresh oregano
¼ cup fresh parsley, chopped
1 teaspoon salt
2 teaspoons black pepper
Lemon wedges for garnish

Directions

1. Combine the cannellini beans, kale, collard greens, red onion, tomato and garlic in a large freezer bag or other storage container.
2. In a bowl combine the vegetable stock, lemon juice, crushed red pepper flakes, oregano, parsley, salt, and black pepper. Mix well.
3. Pour the broth over the beans and greens. Seal tightly and place in the freezer.
4. Serving Day: Remove the contents from the freezer and thaw in the refrigerator for 12 hours or thaw in a microwave on the defrost setting.
5. Pour the contents into a large stock pot. Cook over medium high heat until liquid comes to a boil.
6. Reduce heat to low, cover and simmer for 20 minutes.
7. Serve garnished with fresh lemon wedges, if desired.

Sloppy Lentil Joes

Cook Time: 6 hours - Prep Time: 10 min - Servings: 4-6

Ingredients
2 cups dry lentils
1 cup red onion, diced
3 garlic cloves, crushed and minced
1 cup green bell pepper, diced
1 cup carrots, diced
2 cups tomatoes, diced
4 cups vegetable stock
¼ cup molasses
¼ cup apple cider vinegar
¼ cup tomato paste
2 tablespoons chili powder
1 teaspoon cinnamon
1 teaspoon ground mustard
1 teaspoon salt
1 teaspoon black pepper
Sandwich buns for serving

Directions
1. Combine the lentils, red onion, garlic, green bell pepper, carrots, and tomatoes in a large freezer bag or other storage container.
2. In a bowl combine the vegetable stock, molasses, apple cider vinegar, tomato paste, chili powder, cinnamon, ground mustard, salt, and black pepper. Mix well and add to the lentils.
3. Seal the container tightly and place in the freezer.
4. Serving Day: Remove the contents from the freezer and thaw in the refrigerator for 12 hours or thaw in a microwave on the defrost setting.
5. Place the contents in a slow cooker and cook on low heat for 6 hours or until lentils are tender.
6. Serve on sandwich buns, if desired.

Creamy Squash Casserole

Cook Time: 40 min - Prep Time: 10 min - Servings: 6

Ingredients

4 cups yellow summer squash, sliced
½ cup onion, diced
½ cup poblano pepper, diced
1 cup tomatoes, chopped
2 garlic cloves, crushed and minced
1 cup heavy cream
1 cup parmesan cheese
½ cup feta cheese, crumbled
½ cup seasoned bread crumbs
1 tablespoon fresh dill
1 teaspoon salt
1 teaspoon pepper

Directions

1. Combine the yellow squash, onion, poblano pepper, tomatoes and garlic in a large freezer bag or other storage container. Pour in the heavy cream.
2. In a bowl combine the parmesan cheese, feta cheese, bread crumbs, dill, salt, and pepper. Add to the container and mix with a spoon to incorporate.
3. Seal the container tightly and place in the freezer.
4. Serving Day: Remove the contents from the freezer and thaw in the refrigerator for up to 12 hours or thaw in a microwave on the defrost setting.
5. Preheat the oven to 350°F/177°C.
6. Place the contents in a lightly oiled baking dish. Cover with aluminum foil and bake for 35-40 minutes or until bubbly.
7. Let cool slightly before serving.

Gingered Vegetables

Cook Time: 15 min - Prep Time: 10 min - Servings: 4-6

Ingredients

2 cups broccoli florets

2 cups carrots, sliced

2 cups snow peas

1 cup green beans, trimmed

1 cup celery, diced

1 cup onion, sliced

3 garlic cloves, crushed and minced

1 tablespoon fresh grated ginger

¼ cup soy sauce

¼ cup orange juice

1 tablespoon honey

1 teaspoon crushed red pepper flakes

1 teaspoon salt

1teaspoon black pepper

Cooked rice for serving (optional)

Directions

1. Combine the broccoli, carrots, snow peas, green beans, celery, and onion in a large freezer bag or other storage container.
2. In a bowl combine the garlic, ginger, soy sauce, orange juice, honey, red pepper flakes, salt, and black pepper. Mix well.
3. Add the sauce to the vegetable mixture and seal the container tightly. Place in the freezer.
4. Serving Day: Remove the contents from the freezer and thaw in the refrigerator for 12 hours or thaw in a microwave on the defrost setting.
5. Add the contents to an oiled sauté pan. Cook over medium heat, stirring frequently, for 10-12 minutes or until vegetables are crisp tender.
6. Serve with cooked rice, if desired.

Sweet and Spicy Corn Chowder

Cook Time: 35 min - Prep Time: 10 min - Servings: 4-6

Ingredients

4 cups fresh sweet corn
2 cups jicama, peeled and cubed
1 cup red bell pepper, diced
2 cups carrots, diced
1 cup sweet onion, diced
4 garlic cloves, crushed and minced
1 tablespoon jalapeno pepper, diced
4 cups vegetable stock
1 cup heavy cream
1 teaspoon tarragon
½ teaspoon cayenne powder
1 bay leaf
1 teaspoon salt
1 teaspoon black pepper

Directions

1. Combine the sweet corn, jicama, red bell pepper, carrots, sweet onion, garlic and jalapeno pepper in a large freezer bag or other storage container.
2. In a bowl combine the vegetable stock, heavy cream, tarragon, cayenne powder, bay leaf, salt, and black pepper. Mix well.
3. Pour the creamy mixture over the vegetables.
4. Seal the container tightly and place in the freezer.
5. Serving Day: Remove the contents from the freezer and thaw in the refrigerator for 12 hours or thaw in a microwave on the defrost setting.
6. Add the contents to a large stock pot and cook over medium-high heat until boiling.
7. Reduce the heat to low and simmer for 30 minutes or until the jicama are tender.

Chinese Hot Pot

Cook Time: 20 min - Prep Time: 15 min - Servings: 4-6

Ingredients

1 14-oz package firm tofu, patted dry and cubed
2 cups bok choy, Chopped
2 cups shitake mushrooms, sliced
2 cups edamame, shelled
1 cup carrots, julienned
3 garlic cloves, crushed and minced
1 tablespoon fresh grated ginger
5 cups vegetable stock
1 tablespoon soy sauce
1 tablespoon rice vinegar
1 teaspoon sesame oil
1 whole star anise pod
1 teaspoon coriander
1 tablespoon crushed red pepper flakes
1 teaspoon salt
1 teaspoon black pepper
1 4-oz package rice noodles
Scallions, sliced for garnish

Directions

1. Combine the tofu, bok choy, shitake mushrooms, edamame, and carrots in a large freezer bag or container.
2. In a bowl combine the garlic, ginger, vegetable stock, soy sauce, rice vinegar, and sesame oil. Mix well and season with the star anise, coriander, crushed red pepper flakes, salt, and black pepper.
3. Pour the broth into the container. Seal tightly and place in the freezer.

4. Serving Day: Remove the contents from the freezer and thaw in the refrigerator for 12 hours or thaw in a microwave on the defrost setting.
5. Place the contents into a large stock pot. Cook over medium-high heat until the liquid reaches a gentle boil. Reduce heat to low and simmer for 15 minutes, stirring occasionally.
6. Remove from heat and add the rice noodles. Allow to sit for 5 minutes before serving. Garnish with some thinly sliced scallions, if desired.

Vegetarian Jambalaya

Cook Time: 6 hours - Prep Time: 10 min - Servings: 6-8

Ingredients

2 cups long-grain rice, uncooked
1 cup yellow onion, diced
1 cup green bell pepper, diced
1 cup carrots, diced
1 cup celery, diced
2 cups eggplant, cubed
1 cup zucchini, diced
1 can kidney beans, drained
1 28-oz can stewed tomatoes, liquid reserved
4 garlic cloves, crushed and minced
6 cups vegetable stock
2 cups tomato juice
1 tablespoon fresh thyme
1 teaspoon cayenne powder
1 tablespoon creole seasoning
2 bay leaves
Scallions, sliced for garnish

Directions

1. Place the rice, yellow onion, green bell pepper, carrots, celery, eggplant, zucchini, and kidney beans in a large freezer bag or container.
2. In a large bowl combine the stewed tomatoes, including the liquid, garlic, vegetable stock, tomato juice, thyme, cayenne powder, creole seasoning, and bay leaves. Mix well.
3. Pour the liquid into the container. Seal tightly and place in the freezer.

51

4. Serving Day: Remove the contents from the freezer and thaw in the refrigerator for 12 hours or thaw in a microwave on the defrost setting.
5. Place the contents in a slow cooker and cook for 6-8 hours on low heat.
6. Serve garnished with fresh scallions, if desired.

Tomato Basil Soup

Cook Time: 4 hours - Prep Time: 10 min - Servings: 4-6

Ingredients

4 cups heirloom tomatoes, chopped

1 cup yellow onion, diced

3 garlic cloves, crushed and minced

2 cups vegetable stock

2 cups tomato juice

1 cup heavy cream

1 tablespoon honey

2 cups fresh basil, chopped

1 teaspoon salt

1 teaspoon black pepper

Fresh croutons for garnish

Directions

1. Combine the tomatoes, onion, and garlic in a large freezer bag or other storage container.
2. In a bowl combine the vegetable stock, tomato juice, heavy cream, and honey. Season with the basil, salt, and black pepper. Mix well.
3. Pour the liquid into the bag, seal tightly, and place in the freezer.
4. Serving Day: Remove the contents from the freezer and thaw in the refrigerator for up to 12 hours, or thaw in a microwave on the defrost setting.
5. Place the contents in a slow cooker and cook on low for 4 hours. Leave as a chunky rustic soup, or for a creamier consistency, place half of the contents in a blender and puree until smooth before transferring back into the pot and stirring.
6. Garnish with fresh croutons for serving, if desired.

Dessert Recipes

Triple chocolate brownies

Cook Time: 4 hours - Prep Time: 10 min - Servings: 8-10

Ingredients

1 ¼ cups flour
1 teaspoon baking powder
1 teaspoon salt
3 tablespoons dark cocoa powder
½ teaspoon ground ginger
1 cup white sugar
½ cup butter, melted
1 ½ cups dark chocolate pieces, melted
3 eggs, beaten
1 ½ cups milk chocolate or white chocolate chips

Directions

1. In a bowl combine the flour, baking powder, salt, cocoa powder, and ground ginger.
2. In another bowl combine the sugar, melted butter, melted chocolate, and eggs. Mix until smooth. Gradually incorporate the wet ingredients into the dry, stirring just until blended.
3. Stir in the chocolate chips.
4. Transfer the batter to a large freezer bag or other storage container. Seal tightly and place in the freezer.
5. Serving Day: Place the bag or container in a microwave and thaw on defrost setting.
6. Transfer the batter to a lightly oiled slow cooker. Cook on low for 4 hours.
7. Run a knife along the edge to loosen before serving.

Cherry Vanilla Cobbler

Cook Time: 40 min - Prep Time: 10 min - Servings: 6

Ingredients
2 cups canned cherries
1 cup flour
1 cup white sugar
1 tablespoon baking powder
1 cup heavy cream
½ cup butter, cubed
2 teaspoons pure vanilla extract
1 teaspoon cinnamon
½ teaspoon salt
Fresh cream for serving

Directions
1. Add the cherries to a large freezer bag or other storage container.
2. In a small bowl combine the sugar, flour, and baking powder and add to the cherries. Toss to mix.
3. In another bowl combine the heavy cream, cubed butter, vanilla extract, cinnamon, and salt. Mix well and add to the container. Seal tightly and place in the freezer.
4. Serving Day: Remove the contents from the freezer and thaw in a microwave on the defrost setting.
5. Preheat the oven to 400°F/204°C.
6. Transfer the contents to a lightly oiled 8x8 baking dish.
7. Place in the oven and bake for 30-35 minutes or until bubbly and golden.
8. Drizzle with fresh cream before serving, if desired.

Salted Caramel Everything Bars

Cook Time: 20 min - Prep Time: 10 min - Servings: 12

Ingredients

2 cups almond flour
¼ cup brown sugar
¼ cup butter, melted
1 cup salted pretzel pieces
1 cup pecans, chopped
1 cup dark chocolate chips
1 cup shredded coconut
1 teaspoon coarse salt
1 cup caramel sauce, warmed

Directions

1. In a bowl combine the almond flour, brown sugar, and melted butter. Mix until crumbly.
2. In a large freezer bag or other storage container combine the pretzel pieces, pecans, dark chocolate chips, coconut, and salt. Toss to mix.
3. Add in the flour mixture and toss.
4. Pour in the caramel sauce and stir. Seal the container tightly and place in the freezer.
5. Serving Day: Remove the contents from the freezer and thaw in a microwave on the defrost setting.
6. Preheat oven to 325°F/163°C.
7. Add the contents to a lightly oiled 9"x9" baking dish and pat gently into the bottom.
8. Place the dish in the oven and bake for 20 minutes until golden brown.
9. Let cool before cutting into squares.

Stone Fruit and Nut "Pie"

Cook Time: 6 hours - Prep Time: 10 min - Servings: 8

Ingredients

4 cups peaches, sliced
1 cup plums, sliced
1 cup cherries, pitted and halved
1 cup pecans, chopped
½ cup white sugar
¼ cup brown sugar
2 teaspoons fresh grated ginger
2 teaspoons orange zest
1 teaspoon cinnamon
1 teaspoon vanilla extract
1 frozen pie crust dough, cut into 1 inch pieces
Fresh cream for serving.

Directions

1. In a freezer bag or other storage container combine the peaches, plums, cherries, and pecans.
2. Combine the white and brown sugars and add to the container. Toss to coat the fruit evenly.
3. Add in the ginger, orange zest, cinnamon, vanilla extract, and frozen pie crust pieces. Toss to mix.
4. Seal the container tightly and place in the freezer.
5. Serving Day: Remove the contents from the freezer and thaw in a microwave on the defrost setting.
6. Add the contents to a lightly oiled slow cooker. Cook for 6 hours on low heat.
7. Serve with fresh cream to garnish, if desired.

Recipe Index

More Books by Louise Davidson

Here are some of Louise Davidson's other cookbooks.

Appendix – Cooking Conversion Charts

1. Measuring Equivalent Chart

Type	Imperial	Imperial	Metric
Weight	1 dry ounce		28g
	1 pound	16 dry ounces	0.45 kg
Volume	1 teaspoon		5 ml
	1 dessert spoon	2 teaspoons	10 ml
	1 tablespoon	3 teaspoons	15 ml
	1 Australian tablespoon	4 teaspoons	20 ml
	1 fluid ounce	2 tablespoons	30 ml
	1 cup	16 tablespoons	240 ml
	1 cup	8 fluid ounces	240 ml
	1 pint	2 cups	470 ml
	1 quart	2 pints	0.95 l
	1 gallon	4 quarts	3.8 l
Length	1 inch		2.54 cm

*   Numbers are rounded to the closest equivalent

2. Oven Temperature Equivalent Chart

Fahrenheit (°F)	Celsius (°C)	Gas Mark
220	100	
225	110	1/4
250	120	1/2
275	140	1
300	150	2
325	160	3
350	180	4
375	190	5
400	200	6
425	220	7
450	230	8
475	250	9
500	260	

* Celsius (°C) = T (°F)-32] * 5/9

** Fahrenheit (°F) = T (°C) * 9/5 + 32

*** Numbers are rounded to the closest equivalent

Printed in Great Britain
by Amazon

16058053R00041